FOR THE LOVE OF SPORTS

TRIATHLON

Jessica Coupé

AV2

www.openlightbox.com

AV2

Step 1
Go to **www.openlightbox.com**

Step 2
Enter this unique code

WSFOK7HDI

Step 3
Explore your interactive eBook!

AV2 is optimized for use on any device

Your interactive eBook comes with...

Contents
Browse a live contents page to easily navigate through resources

Audio
Listen to sections of the book read aloud

Videos
Watch informative video clips

Weblinks
Gain additional information for research

Slideshows
View images and captions

Try This!
Complete activities and hands-on experiments

Key Words
Study vocabulary, and complete a matching word activity

Quizzes
Test your knowledge

Share
Share titles within your Learning Management System (LMS) or Library Circulation System

Citation
Create bibliographical references following APA, CMOS, and MLA styles

This title is part of our AV2 digital subscription

1-Year Grades K–5 Subscription
ISBN 978-1-7911-3320-7

Access hundreds of AV2 titles with our digital subscription.
Sign up for a FREE trial at **www.openlightbox.com/trial**

FOR THE LOVE OF SPORTS

TRIATHLON

CONTENTS

What Is Triathlon?

A triathlon is an **endurance** race that involves swimming, cycling, and running over different distances. The winner is the competitor, or triathlete, who finishes the race first. Triathlon began in the 1970s in San Diego, California. Athletes Jack Johnstone and Don Shanahan organized a new type of race. The 46 participants swam 500 yards (457 meters), ran 6 miles (9.7 kilometers) and cycled 5 miles (8 km). One of the participants was a U.S. Navy officer named John Collins.

Triathlon has been open to both men and women since the sport began.

A few years later, Collins created a triathlon of his own. As he was living in Hawaii, he called the event the Hawaiian Ironman triathlon. Whoever finished first would be called the "Iron Man."

Today, more than 6 million athletes participate in triathlons worldwide. There are almost 100 national federations globally. Triathlons are supported by an international federation, called World Triathlon. Triathlon competitions are held in a wide range of distances.

Triathlon athletes need to be strong and have good stamina.

About 8,000 triathletes attended the Noosa Triathlon Multisport Festival in 2015, making it one of the biggest triathlons in the world.

The best triathletes can complete an Olympic-distance triathlon in under 2 hours.

Ironman Triathlon participants travel more than 140 miles (225 km) before reaching the finish line.

Getting Ready to Play

Each **segment** of a triathlon requires specific equipment and clothing. These items help improve performance and ensure an athlete's safety. Triathletes need swimming, cycling, and running gear.

Participants in a triathlon must wear a number that is always visible. For longer races, triathletes have transition gear, which keeps them prepared for each stage. The gear includes a transition bag for easy access when switching between segments. In the bag, triathletes have a towel, shoes, and bicycle helmet.

Swimming goggles protect a triathlete's eyes from saltwater and other irritants. They also help triathletes with underwater vision.

A triathlon bike is designed for speed. It has **aerodynamic** features such as its frame and handlebars. These help the triathlete cycle quickly.

A helmet is a mandatory piece of equipment during the cycling section of a triathlon.

A trisuit is a one-piece suit. It is designed to allow triathletes to participate in the swim, bike, and run segments without having to change clothing.

Triathlon shoes are lightweight to provide comfort and support. Bicycling shoes are stiff and clip onto bicycle pedals. Some have holes to drain water from the swimming section. Triathletes may also have separate running shoes with quick laces that do not need to be tied.

A **timing chip** is worn on each triathlete's ankle. It records the athlete's time throughout the event.

The Triathlon Course

The size of a triathlon course varies according to the distance triathletes have to cover during the race. However, there are always three segmented areas and two transition stations. The first segmented area is typically the shortest part of the race. Triathletes may have to swim in a lake, river, sea, or even a pool. Colored **buoys** mark the course.

Once swimmers make it to shore, they go to the first transition station. This is an area where they can change out of their swimsuits and into a trisuit if needed. They also pick up their bicycles for the next segment of the race. The bicycle segment is often over steep, hilly roads. At its end, triathletes go to the second transition station. Many change to running shoes. The running segment is sometimes the hardest to complete, as muscles are tired from the previous segments.

Triathlon Championships

Major triathlon events are held around the world. These include Olympic competitions and other events organized by groups such as World Triathlon. Some individual events are known worldwide, such as the Escape from Alcatraz Triathlon. This event includes a 1.5-mile (2.4-km) swim, followed by an 18-mile (29-km) bike, then an 8-mile (13-km) run. About 2,000 **amateur** and **professional** triathletes take part in the event.

San Francisco, California

The Escape from Alcatraz course starts on a ferry near the former prison on Alcatraz Island. Triathletes jump off the ferry into the cold waters and swim for shore. They then cycle and run the rest of the course.

Keeping Score

In an individual triathlon, the winner is the triathlete who crosses the finish line first. The first three places are called **podium** finishes. The fastest triathlete earns gold. Second place is silver, and third is bronze.

A triathlon can be part of an official triathlon series. One example is the World Triathlon Championship Series. Triathletes earn points for how well they do in each triathlon they complete. At the end of the season, the triathlete with the most total points wins.

Before a run, triathletes develop their strategy carefully. They plan how to run or hike up the hills. Then, they use the energy saved to make up time when they go downhill.

A series of triathlons may take place all over the world. The World Triathlon Championship Series is made up of seven to nine annual World Championship Triathlons, including the Olympics if they take place that year. As athletes compete in more races, they keep adding the points they earn from each race to their total scores.

Triathletes pace themselves during the cycling race so they still have energy for the run.

One triathlon swimming strategy is to start slow and then speed up in the second half of the section. This allows a triathlete to pass competitors who started by swimming too quickly.

Rules of the Contest

Several rules help a triathlon go smoothly. Triathletes must follow the course route. They must also follow directions from race officials. Competitors cannot receive aid from anyone other than the race staff, medical staff, and volunteers.

In the bicycling portion of the race, triathletes are not allowed to cycle without cycling shoes. They also must wear safety-approved bicycle helmets. In some races, **drafting** is not allowed. This creates space between triathletes during the cycling portion of the event, making them less likely to bump into each other.

Most races require triathletes to mark their race number on their leg and arm. These numbers help identify triathletes as they transition between segments of the race.

As triathletes participate in the race, they may be penalized for breaking rules. Colored cards indicate how severe a penalty is. A yellow card means a 10- or 60-second penalty. A blue card, given for drafting, means a 5-minute penalty. If triathletes litter, they also receive a 5-minute penalty. Triathletes are not allowed to wear music players or other devices that would cause them to miss instructions from officials. In individual triathlons, when triathletes cross the finish line, they hand their timing chip to an official to record their time.

Triathletes must wear wetsuits for the swim segment if the water is 65 degrees Fahrenheit (18 degrees Celsius) or lower in temperature.

If triathletes fail to keep their helmets on until the cycling portion of the race is completed, they receive a penalty.

In relay races, teams are made of two or three athletes. Each competes in different segments of the race.

Competing

Many triathletes around the world take part in amateur competitions. Some of the most popular types of triathlons are the Super Sprint, the Sprint, the Olympic Distance, the Triathlon 70.3, and the Ironman Triathlon. Each one is of a different length, which sets its level of difficulty and the amount of time it takes to complete.

Many triathlon organizations sponsor junior triathlons for children.

Amateurs can expect to finish an Olympic Distance triathlon in about 2 to 5 hours.

USA Triathlon is the governing body for triathlons in the United States. It is one of the largest multi-sport organizations in the world. The organization sanctions about 3,500 events and races for more than 300,000 members each year. Popular USA Triathlon events include the Chicago Triathlon, which features races for beginners, children, the elderly, and professional triathletes.

World Triathlon is the international governing body of both triathlon and other multisports events. The major triathlon events it regulates include the Ironman, World Triathlon Championship series, Pan American Games, and the Olympic and **Paralympic** Games.

Paralympic triathlons include a 820-yard (750-m) swim, 12.4-mile (20-km) cycling course, and 3.1-mile (5-km) run.

There are many different multisports similar to triathlon, including **duathlon**, **aquathlon**, aquabike, winter triathlon, off-road triathlon, and paratriathlon.

History of Triathlon

People have been competing in races with three segments since the early 1900s. Over the years, the distance for each of the segments has increased. Many people have enjoyed watching triathlons and participating in them as a test of endurance.

The first Hawaiian Ironman Triathlon only had 15 participants. Today, more than 2,000 athletes from 50 countries take part in this event.

1920s In France, a race called *Les Trois Sports*, or "The Three Sports," is held. It features running, swimming, and bicycling.

1974 The first official triathlon is held. Taking place in Mission Bay, it includes a 5.3-mile (8.5 km) run, a 5-mile (8-km) cycle, and a swim of almost 600 yards (550 m).

1978 The first Ironman Triathlon is held in Honolulu, Hawaii. Gordon Haller, a taxi driver, becomes the first "Iron Man," finishing in just under 12 hours.

1989 The International Triathlon Union (ITU) is founded in Avignon, France. The first World Championship Triathlon is also held.

2000 Triathlon becomes an Olympic sport at the Summer Olympics in Sydney, Australia.

2024 At the Summer Olympics in Paris, France, 55 men and 55 women compete in three triathlon events. These are the men's individual triathlon, women's individual triathlon, and mixed relay.

The first triathlon to be televised was the 1980 Ironman Triathlon.

Para triathlon was first included in the Paralympic Games in 2016.

Born in 1998, Taylor Knibb is the youngest female U.S. Olympic triathlete.

Superstars of Triathlon

There are many notable triathletes, both modern and from the sport's early days.

Erin Baker

BIRTH DATE: May 23, 1961
HOMETOWN: Kaiapoi, New Zealand

CAREER FACTS:

- Erin won first place in the Elite Women category in the first World Triathlon Championship in 1989.
- Erin was named "Triathlete of the Decade" by *Triathlete* magazine.
- Erin was made a Member of the Order of the British Empire (MBE) for her triathlete career.
- Between 1985 and 1994, Erin placed first in 10 of the 14 triathlons she ran.
- Erin won a total of 104 of the 121 races she entered.

Kristian Blumenfelt

BIRTH DATE: February 14, 1994
HOMETOWN: Bergen, Norway

CAREER FACTS:

- In 2018, Kristian had four podium finishes in the ITU World Triathlon Series. He won three silver medals and one bronze.
- In 2021, Kristian made history by winning the World Triathlon Championship Series, the Olympic Triathlon, and the Ironman World Championship in the same year.
- In 2022, Kristian won the Ironman World Championship race in St. George, Utah, and set the world record for the fastest Ironman race at the Pho3nix Sub7 event in Phoenix, Arizona.

Alistair Brownlee

BIRTH DATE: April 23, 1988
HOMETOWN: Dewsbury, England

CAREER FACTS:

- In 2014, Alistair won the European title in Kitzbühel, Austria.
- Alistair is a two-time Olympic triathlon champion.
- At the 2016 Olympic Games, Alistair won gold, finishing 6 seconds ahead of his younger brother, Jonathan.
- Alistair also won two golds at the **Commonwealth Games** in Glasgow.

Beth Potter

BIRTH DATE: December 27, 1991
HOMETOWN: Glasgow, Scotland

CAREER FACTS:

- Beth won a bronze medal in triathlon at the 2022 Commonwealth Games.
- In 2023, Beth earned the World Triathlon Championship title by winning the series final in Pontevedra, Spain.
- Beth was named Scottish Sportswoman of the Year in 2023.
- Beth won three bronze medals in 2024. One was at the World Triathlon Championship Series Hamburg, and two were at the Olympics.

Jonathan Brownlee

BIRTH DATE: April 30, 1990
HOMETOWN: Leeds, England

CAREER FACTS:

- Jonathan was World Triathlon Champion in 2012.
- At the 2016 Olympic Games, Jonathan won silver, finishing behind his brother, Alistair. This marked the first time two brothers had won gold and silver in the Individual triathlon at the Olympics.
- Jonathan is a three-time Olympic medalist, making him the most decorated in triathlon Olympic history.

Cassandre Beaugrand

BIRTH DATE: May 23, 1997
HOMETOWN: Livry-Gargan, France

CAREER FACTS:

- In 2022, Cassandre won the World Championship Mixed Relay in Montreal Quebec .
- Cassandre won gold at the 2024 Paris Olympics.
- Cassandre set an Olympic record for the 6-mile (10-km) run.
- Cassandre won the Women's Individual at the World Series in 2024 in Hamburg.

Alex Yee

BIRTH DATE: February 18, 1998
HOMETOWN: Lewisham, London, England

CAREER FACTS:

- Alex won two medals at the Olympic Games held in Tokyo in 2021. He earned a silver in the Individual and gold in the Mixed Relay.
- Alex received one gold and one silver medal at the 2024 Paris Olympic Games.
- In 2024, Alex won the World Triathlon Championship.

Staying Healthy

Exercise, such as swimming, bicycling, and running, helps keep triathletes strong and healthy. Eating a balanced diet also helps. Without good nutrition, triathletes will not have the strength to finish a triathlon. Triathletes eat **protein**, such as meat. This aids muscle recovery and boosts their immune system. Carbohydrates, such as brown rice, quinoa, and bananas, provide energy before events.

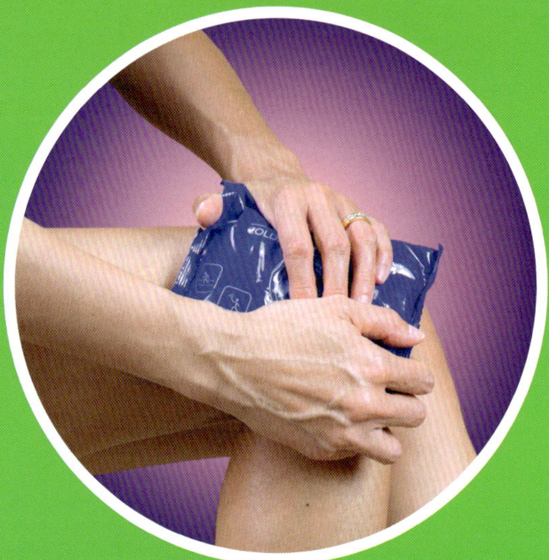

Triathletes suffer from strained muscles. They put ice packs on these areas to prevent inflammation and ease the pain.

Before a race, triathletes often have small, high-energy breakfasts, such as peanut butter sandwiches.

Staying **hydrated** is also very important for triathletes during and after a competition. Drinking water helps athletes prevent injury by cushioning their joints and keeping their body temperature regulated. Those who do not drink enough water risk tiring their muscles and losing coordination when they race.

Strong muscles are needed to compete in the triathlon. Triathletes train to improve their swimming, bicycling, and running times. How often they train depends on the race they are training for.

Triathletes need to have strong legs during the triathlon. Some triathletes will do an exercise called a lunge. This movement helps them strengthen their legs and improve their balance. Triathletes perform squats to strengthen their legs as well. They also do push-ups to build up muscles in their arms and hands.

Some triathletes may train for hours every day before a triathlon. It is important to develop enough endurance to complete all three parts of the event.

THE TRIATHLON QUIZ

- 1 -

Where was the **first** Ironman Triathlon held?

- 2 -

What are the three different **sports** in a triathlon?

- 3 -

What year did the triathlon become an **Olympic Sport**?

- 4 -

The triathlon is a **test** of what?

- 5 -

What must cyclists wear during the **bike** part of the race?

- 6 -

What is the international **governing body** of triathlon?

- 7 -

Who won the women's **triathlon event** at the 2024 Paris Olympics?

- 8 -

What do triathletes hand to an **official** after they finish the race?

- 9 -

What is typically the **shortest portion** of a triathlon?

- 10 -

Which exercises do triathletes do to **strengthen** their legs?

ANSWERS: 1 Honolulu, Hawaii 2 Swimming, cycling, running 3 2000 4 Endurance 5 A helmet 6 World Triathlon 7 Cassandre Beaugrand 8 Timing chip 9 Swimming 10 Lunges and squats

Key Words

aerodynamic: made or moving in a way that moves through air easily

amateur: taking part in something for fun

aquathlon: a race in which competitors swim, then run

buoys: floating objects at the surface of a body of water, used to direct people and ships

Commonwealth Games: an international sporting event in which most competing nations are former British territories

drafting: when a competitor rides, swims, or runs closely behind another athlete to save energy and maintain speed

duathlon: a race in which competitors run, then cycle, then run again

endurance: in racing, an event that takes place over a long distance or time

hydrated: having replaced water in the body through drinking or eating

Paralympic: relating to a series of international contests for athletes with disabilities

podium: in sports, a raised platform used when presenting awards to the top three competitors in an event

professional: taking part in an activity or sport as a job

protein: complex compounds found in foods such as meat

segment: an individual part of something

timing chip: an electronic device that attaches to an athlete and records his or her time at the start and finish of a race

Index

Get the best of both worlds.

AV2 bridges the gap between print and digital.

The expandable resources toolbar enables quick access to content including videos, audio, activities, **weblinks**, **slideshows**, **quizzes**, and **key words**.

Animated videos make static images come alive.

Resource icons on each page help readers to further **explore key concepts**.

Published by Lightbox Learning Inc.
276 5th Avenue, Suite 704 #917
New York, NY 10001
Website: www.openlightbox.com

Library of Congress Control Number: 2025931414

ISBN 979-8-8745-2654-2 (hardcover)
ISBN 979-8-8745-2655-9 (softcover)
ISBN 979-8-8745-2656-6 (static multi-user eBook)
ISBN 979-8-8745-2658-0 (interactive multi-user eBook)

Printed in Guangzhou, China
1 2 3 4 5 6 7 8 9 0 29 28 27 26 25

012025
101124

Project Coordinator John Willis
Art Director Terry Paulhus
Layout Jean Faye Rodriguez

Photo Credits
Every reasonable effort has been made to trace ownership and to obtain permission to reprint copyright material. The publisher would be pleased to have any errors or omissions brought to its attention so that they may be corrected in subsequent printings. The publisher acknowledges Alamy, Getty Images, and Shutterstock as its primary image suppliers for this title.